Gallery Books
Editor Peter Fallon

SKY ROAD

Jim Nolan

SKY ROAD

Gallery Books

Sky Road
was first published
simultaneously in paperback
and in a clothbound edition
on the day of its première
15 October 2007.

The Gallery Press
Loughcrew
Oldcastle
County Meath
Ireland

www.gallerypress.com

© Jim Nolan 2007

ISBN 978 1 85235 390 2 *paperback*
     978 1 85235 391 9 *clothbound*

A CIP catalogue record for this book
is available from the British Library.

Characters

FRANK CONROY, TD
KATHERINE, *his wife*
TESS, *their daughter*
STEPHEN, *their son*
JOHNNY, *their younger son*
JOE HARRINGTON, *a journalist*

Time and Place

ACT ONE
A summer evening, in the early 1980s.

ACT TWO
A winter night. Four years later.

The Conroy home overlooking the sea on the outskirts of the village of Seafield on the south coast of Ireland.

Sky Road was first produced in the Theatre Royal, Waterford, on Monday, 15 October 2007, with the following cast (in order of appearance):

KATHERINE	Marion O'Dwyer
TESS	Judith Roddy
JOE	Charlie Bonner
JOHNNY	Colin O'Donoghue
CONROY	Barry McGovern
STEPHEN	Keith McErlean

Direction	Ben Barnes
Design	Dermot Quinn
Lighting Design	Nick McCall
Costume Design	Therese McKeone, Sinéad Cuthbert
Sound Design	Jamie Beamish

for my mother, Alice

ACT ONE

Scene One

The verandah of the Conroy family home on a summer evening in the early 1980s. The house overlooks the sea on the outskirts of the village of Seafield on the south coast. Lights come up on an empty space. After a moment the double doors leading to the house swing open. KATHERINE *and* TESS *emerge,* TESS *carrying bunting and* KATHERINE *a silver tray of champagne glasses which she places on a trestle table laden with plates, bowls, cutlery and finger food.*

KATHERINE (*As she enters*) I have many gifts, Tess! Bilocation, regrettably, isn't yet one of them!

TESS Then you should have travelled with Da.

KATHERINE Talk about the pot calling the kettle black! At least *I* went to Dublin.

TESS (*Preparing to hang bunting*) You sure did. And came home in the back of Joe Harrington's jalopy when you should have been travelling in style with our new Minister.

KATHERINE (*As she sets and arranges table*) I'm sure there was many the night you were glad of the same back seat.

TESS Mother!

KATHERINE Deny it if you will! The sooner your fiancé makes a decent woman of you the better. And besides, it's far from State Mercs I was reared.

TESS Well, you'd better get used to it.

KATHERINE I'm sure I will! And your father won't starve for company. He has half the Constituency Party in cavalcade behind him. And far from deserting him, young lady, I came on ahead with Joe to look after this.

TESS   I told you I'd take care of this.

KATHERINE   Just like I told *you* any one of the Party faithful could have organized the victory rally. But Miss Bossy Boots had to do it all by herself — and miss the greatest day of her father's life in the process.

TESS   I was there in spirit. Unlike some I could mention, I'm not a kept woman! I had a class to teach.

KATHERINE   Ever hear of a day off?

TESS   No. And as for that rally, just because I organized it doesn't mean I've changed my opinion. I still think it's a mistake.

KATHERINE   I *know* what you think.

TESS   You know what our new Minister thinks too.

KATHERINE   What your father *wants* is one thing, Tess. What he *needs* is quite another! How did you get on anyway?

TESS   Not bad for four hours' notice.

KATHERINE   I don't know why it couldn't have been arranged before today.

TESS   Same reason you didn't have *this* ready in advance. Wouldn't we look the right eejits if Da didn't get the nod!

KATHERINE   It was never in doubt!

TESS   That's not what I heard.

KATHERINE   Strut and posturing! Testosterone wafting from the Party Room all morning.

TESS   They say Grogan tried to back-pedal on the deal he made with Dad.

KATHERINE   Are we surprised?

TESS   Hardly.

KATHERINE   Summoning all the oratorical power for which our new Taoiseach is justly famous he told your father and the other 'dissenters', as he refers to them, that an Anti-Corruption Commission 'would be the equivalent of washing the Party's underpants on the lawn of Leinster House'!

TESS   A charming prospect.

KATHERINE   Indeed!

TESS   But our Minstrel Boy faced him down.

KATHERINE I met him in Buswells for a few minutes during the stand-off. I've never seen him look as tired or as resolute, Tess. No Commission, no deal! And Grogan blinked! Ten minutes before going into the Chamber for the vote he sent for your father and the others and signed off — not just on this Anti-Corruption thingamajig, but on a string of policy commitments that would put a card-carrying socialist to shame.

TESS I wouldn't put much store by Emmet Grogan's promises. That man would sign his mother's death warrant for a shot at power.

KATHERINE Who are you telling? But it's a start, Tess — a new beginning.

TESS I hope so.

KATHERINE O ye of little faith! Francis Conroy, TD — Minister for the Environment! It does have a certain ring to it, doesn't it?

TESS (*Smiling*) I suppose it does.

JOE HARRINGTON *enters. He carries a large banner which he drops to the floor before embracing* TESS.

JOE Salutations, Tessie! (*He kisses her*) Did you miss me?

TESS (*Laughing*) I survived.

JOE Do you mind her, Katherine? Girl goes into decline if I cross the county border for more than twenty minutes. You missed a great day, Tess.

TESS (*Lightly*) From what I hear you made the most of it.

KATHERINE First official duty of the new Minister. Signing his future son-in-law here into the Dáil bar.

JOE *One* drink for the day was in it. And purely for research. Isn't that right, Katherine?

KATHERINE That's what makes you such a good journalist, Joe.

JOE I couldn't agree more. (*Banner*) Right, one 'Welcome Home' sign, ink barely dry! Where do you want it, girls?

TESS Try over the door. And sometime *today*, if you

don't mind — they'll be here in a minute.

KATHERINE (*As* JOE *climbs the ladder to hang the banner*) Not if the crowd of diehards on Strand Bridge get their way. They'll want a speech at least, if not an outright Declaration of Independence. I saw one old dear with a musty old portrait of Grogan in one hand and — wait for it, Tess — a picture of the Sacred Heart in the other!

JOE Maybe the Minister will perform a miracle on the way.

KATHERINE He won't have time. Victory rally in the Square in Rathmore at eight sharp! They'll have to settle for a Ministerial wave in the meantime.

TESS Miracles are a little harder to come by, aren't they?

Silence.

KATHERINE You promised you wouldn't do this, Tess. (TESS *does not respond*) Do you think any of us have forgotten what's happened? Do you think your father has? Laura Gavin was his Clinic secretary, — he knows her better than any of us.

TESS All the more reason why this victory parade mightn't be such a good idea.

KATHERINE What happened to Laura and your brother was a terrible accident. No one needs reminding of that. But your father has waited thirty-six years for this night. And nothing gives anyone the right to take it away from him.

TESS Not even Laura dying?

KATHERINE The doctors say she may still come round. We have to believe that. But it will be three weeks tomorrow — We don't have the privilege of putting our lives on hold while we wait for Laura to get better.

TESS She isn't *getting* better.

KATHERINE We don't know that. (*Pause*) But here's something I do know. I watched your father leaving Leinster House today on his way to the President. He looked

like the loneliest man on earth, Tess — on what
should have been the greatest day of his life.

TESS I won't let him down.

KATHERINE You never have. (*Turning to* JOE) Which is more
than can be said for the impartial reporter above
on the ladder. That banner is leaning to the left,
Joe.

JOE Just like your husband.

TESS (*Smiling at* JOE) I'll get the champagne.

TESS *exits.*

JOE (*Descending ladder*) Are you okay?

KATHERINE (*Smiles*) No.

JOE If it's any consolation, you're playing a blinder.

KATHERINE That's not what it feels like.

JOE Then you'll just have to take my word for it.

KATHERINE I don't have a heart of stone, Joe.

JOE I know you don't.

KATHERINE Any chance you'd tell that to your fiancée?

JOE I don't need to.

KATHERINE But you think she might have a point about this
rally?

JOE It's a tough call.

KATHERINE It wasn't made lightly. I'm as close to Laura as any
of them, Joe.

JOE I know that.

KATHERINE When Frank took her on I confess it was against
my better judgement. One hundred words a
minute is one thing, but a seventeen-year-old
child who'd never stepped beyond the walls of an
orphanage —

JOE Frank was always a soft touch.

KATHERINE Who are you telling? She'll be fine, he said — and
he was right. All those petty reservations went
flying out the window the first time I saw her. I love
her just like they do, Joe. But this rally — it's more
than some lap of honour. They *need* to see him
home. And he *needs* them, too — more than he

15

knows. (*Pause*) You shouldn't have to listen to this.

JOE It's alright. Anyway, amn't I almost one of the family?

KATHERINE A dubious distinction right now. (*Pause*) Have you seen Stephen?

JOE I called round to his pub a few times. Young lad that works for him said he gives day and night at the hospital.

KATHERINE So I hear.

JOE I called by there one night. Told him I was around if he wanted to talk.

KATHERINE And?

JOE He said there was nothing to talk about and asked me to leave. Nobody's blaming him for what happened, Katherine.

KATHERINE Not yet. But if Laura dies — Tess is right — she isn't getting better.

JOE One way or the other it was still an accident. That car crash wasn't the first on the Sky Road and it won't be the last.

KATHERINE You're his best friend, Joe. I know he never made that easy, but you'll stand by him, won't you?

JOE Goes without saying. Just like it goes without saying Tess will be there when it counts for our new Minister.

KATHERINE I know. And she'll need to be. If this Anti-Corruption Commission of his is given the teeth to do its work —

JOE Your belovèd leader, Grogan, will be the first to come under the spotlight. We hardly need a Commission to tell us what he's been up to.

KATHERINE No. But we'd need one to prove it. Everybody knows what's under the stones, Joe — but no one's ever dared lift them. Trouble is it won't just be Grogan. Frank broke ranks today and they weren't queuing up in the Dáil bar to thank him for it.

JOE So I noticed. He won't care. You know that.

KATHERINE I know. When my husband believes in something

he just puts his head down and goes for it —
whatever the cost.

JOE   (*Smiling*) A fatal flaw in a politician.

KATHERINE   A fatal flaw in any of us.

JOHNNY *enters.*

JOHNNY   Howya, Ma?

KATHERINE   Johnny! What in God's name are you doing here?

JOHNNY   I am about my father's business!

KATHERINE   Last time I saw you you were leaving the Dáil to
go back to College. In case it slipped your mind,
you sit your Finals next week.

JOHNNY   And in case it slipped yours, I'm studying Politics.
You find me a textbook that'll teach half what I
learnt today and I'll swallow it whole — hardback
cover an' all! One night, Ma. You wouldn't
begrudge your favourite son the victory rally,
would you?

KATHERINE   (*Smiling*) No. I suppose not.

TESS *returns with a bottle of champagne in ice
bucket.*

JOHNNY   Howya doin', sis?

TESS   Hi, Johnny. Did you have a good day?

JOHNNY   It was rock and roll! I just about stopped short of
giving interviews to the Press about the State of
the Nation. I even got to chinwag with the new
Taoiseach.

TESS   A memorable encounter, no doubt.

JOHNNY   (*Mimics Grogan*) 'I can't tell you how much I look
forward to working with your father,' says he. 'I
bet you can't,' says I, 'ye slippery oul' shite!'

KATHERINE   (*Enjoying this*) You did not!

JOHNNY   Under my breath, of course.

TESS   (*Laughing*) How did you get here, Johnny?

JOHNNY   I rode shotgun in the State car with the Minister.
No disrespect to your old banger, Joe, but it's the

only way to travel!

JOE I'll take your word for it.

KATHERINE Where *is* your father?

JOHNNY The cavalcade was waylaid at the edge of the village. 'To hell with the fancy Merc,' they said. 'We carried him to Dublin and we'll carry him home!' Horsed him out of the car, they did, and ferried him shoulder high up the Green Road to the Bridge, one batin' the other off for the honour and glory of it. Big Blaise Power with his veins poppin', Tommy Goggin with his gimpy leg, Sam Dowling, only six weeks over a triple bypass and the big puss on him like a traffic light stuck on red. The last I saw of Da he was above on the parapet the far side of Strand Bridge, performing what looked suspiciously like a re-enactment of the Civil War. (*Pause*) He can sure turn it on when he wants to, though. Hardly spoke the whole way down and then lets loose as if his life depended on it.

KATHERINE Your father knows where his bread is buttered. It'll warm him up nicely for the rally.

JOHNNY I suppose so. Is Stephen here?

TESS He's at the hospital.

JOHNNY How's Laura?

TESS The same. I'm sure Stephen would be glad to see you.

KATHERINE Johnny's only just back, Tess. Maybe he could go later.

JOHNNY (*Looking at* TESS) I'll go out after the rally. Speaking of which, what's the drill, Ma?

KATHERINE Assuming Sam Dowling doesn't keel over and have another coronary, the Minister should be here shortly. There'll be just about time for our little welcome home and then it's on to Rathmore for the parade. Torchlight entrance into the Square, the Knockmahon Pipe Band belting out 'The Minstrel Boy' for all their worth — with the Minister and ourselves above on Flahavan's flat truck, wavin' to the crowds like soldiers from the wars returning.

JOHNNY The business! I might say the *cúpla focal* myself if the spirit moves me.

TESS You will not. I have the running order and it does *not* include you.

JOHNNY Only joking, Tess. But it might not be too long before it does.

TESS How d'you mean?

JOHNNY Stop Press, Joe! Da says he wants to talk to me about his seat on the Council. You might just be looking at the next generation of the Conroy dynasty.

JOE I didn't think your father was obliged to resign his seat.

KATHERINE He isn't. But I should think he'll have enough to occupy him.

JOHNNY And if he does go, it'll fall to the Party to co-opt his successor. I knew all those boring Cumann meetings above in UCD would stand to me some day.

KATHERINE I wouldn't count my chickens just yet if I were you. Even if your father *does* resign it doesn't follow you'll be nominated.

JOHNNY Custom and practice in the Party, Ma. The departing Chief names the heir to his throne.

TESS Except the heir hasn't been named, has he?

JOHNNY (*A glance to* KATHERINE) Stephen passed on all this a long time ago. I know everybody would like that to be otherwise, but it's not my fault he didn't make it.

CONROY *has arrived in the house.*

CONROY (*Off*) Anybody home?

KATHERINE Jesus, Mary and Joseph, he's here!

Ushers the others into position to greet CONROY.

Stand by, everybody!

CONROY *enters and stands framed in the double doors — at once surprised and embarrassed by the welcoming party.*

Ladies and Gentlemen, I give you, the new Minister for the Environment — and the promise of a better tomorrow: Mr Francis Conroy, TD!

KATHERINE *applauds heartily. The others follow, uncertain what form the ceremony should take.*

Welcome home, Frank!

CONROY Thank you. It's been an eventful day. None of it means more than this.

TESS (*Embracing her father*) Congratulations, Minister. I knew I could leave you off on your own.

CONROY Don't make a habit of it.

TESS I won't.

CONROY I'd have thought you'd have had your fill of all this pomp and ceremony by now, Joe.

JOE It's not often it happens.

CONROY That might not be a bad thing.

TESS A hard day at the office, I hear.

CONROY I wouldn't say that. The Taoiseach and I had what is described in all the best communiqués as a 'frank exchange of views'.

TESS We heard it was a bit more than that.

CONROY Then you heard what he wanted you to hear. Our revered Party Leader was never going back to the Opposition benches. We both knew that. What happened this morning was just a necessary ritual.

KATHERINE The Dance of the Huckabees! Now come on — I've been waiting all day to see it.

CONROY See what?

KATHERINE Don't be so modest! Your Seal of Office.

CONROY You'll be lucky. Some Civil Servant functionary snatched them from our fists as soon as the President left the room.

KATHERINE That's a bit ungracious!

CONROY Maybe they figure we won't need them for long.

KATHERINE Nonsense! They can have the Seal — but not the Office! Your father would have been so proud of you today. A man that gave his every waking breath to the Party, Johnny. Twenty-three years on the back benches!

JOHNNY (*Laughing*) I know the family history, Ma.

KATHERINE You didn't know John Conroy! Revered by his own the same as your father. Would have scaled the side of a mountain with a blindfold and one leg to get a vote out, Joe, but the top brass would hardly remember his name until the Division bells rang. I bet he sang in his grave today.

CONROY I'm sure he did. (*Pause*) Was there any news from the hospital, Tess?

TESS There's no change.

CONROY And Stephen?

TESS I haven't seen him.

KATHERINE Stephen is bearing up, Frank. (*Approaching table*) Now, come on — we don't have much time.

CONROY Is this in my honour?

JOHNNY (*Eternal patience*) No, Da. Emmet Grogan said he might drop by for a cup of tea and a chat. Who do you think it's for!

CONROY I'm very grateful. To all of you.

TESS Johnny-come-lately here had nothing to do with it, so you needn't go thanking him. Joe hung the banner — all by himself, as is probably obvious. The rest is down to your loving wife.

CONROY Thank you, Katherine.

KATHERINE You're more than welcome, Minister. We just wanted five minutes with you before we give you away for the next five years. Now I'm not in the habit of speechifying in our own backyard but tonight I'm going to make an exception!

TESS Shouldn't we wait for Stephen?

KATHERINE (*Beat*) We don't have time.

CONROY Maybe we should make time. I'd like him to be here.

KATHERINE   Which is why I invited him. But he isn't here
            and I doubt if he's coming now. This isn't about
            Stephen, Frank. This is about *you*. About a politi-
            cal lifetime shouting down a dark corridor and
            nobody listening. Well, they're listening now.
            Whatever Emmet Grogan was up to today, you
            were fighting for what kind of country we get to
            live in for the next five years. And you *won*, Frank.
            I just wanted to mark that in case the moment
            slipped by unnoticed.

CONROY   I'm sorry. Maybe we do owe ourselves this. One
            night before the real war starts.

JOHNNY   You'll be well able for Grogan, Da.

CONROY   You think so?

KATHERINE   Never a truer word was spoken! Now, are we
            going to drink that champagne or pray to it? Do
            the honours, Joe — a quick glass for everybody
            and then it's on to Rathmore where the faithful
            await!

TESS   (*As* JOE *uncorks bottle and pours the champagne which*
            TESS *will distribute over following sequence*) Speaking
            of whom — we had a distinguished visitor to the
            Constituency Office today, Da.

CONROY   Who was that?

TESS   Paddy Brennan.

CONROY   (*Beat*) What did *he* want?

TESS   He'd just heard about your appointment and asked
            me to convey his 'warmest congratulations'.

CONROY   The Judas kiss if ever there was one.

KATHERINE   Now Frank — I'm sure he meant well!

CONROY   I'm sure he did. I added an item of local interest to
            the shopping list Grogan signed off on today. If I
            know Brennan his 'courtesy call' wasn't entirely
            unconnected to it.

JOHNNY   What was it, Da — Sam Dowling for President?!

KATHERINE   (*Laughing*) Be quiet, Johnny.

CONROY   Kilgallen House is coming on the market in the
            next few weeks. Grogan damn near choked on his
            morning coffee when I told him I wanted the

OPW to bid for the estate at the auction.

JOHNNY What's his problem? I'd have thought Grogan would enjoy reclaiming our native heath from the Saxon foe!

CONROY In other circumstances, maybe.

JOE But not when one of your Party's leading benefactors happens to have his eye on the same property.

CONROY Full marks, Joe.

JOE Hardly. The dogs in the street have been barking it since the 'For Sale' signs were posted. (*To* TESS) Apparently Brennan's old man worked on the estate back in the Fifties. Word is he wants to buy it for sentimental reasons.

CONROY I can assure you Brennan's interest in four hundred acres of land overlooking the sea is far from sentimental.

KATHERINE What's *your* interest, Frank?

CONROY (*Stung*) A nineteenth-century house crying out for restoration. An estate that would make a fine Community Park.

JOHNNY You could do without making an enemy of Paddy Brennan, Da.

CONROY He *is* my enemy.

JOHNNY He's also the biggest employer in this constituency. How many enemies can you afford?

TESS Brennan's not the only one brought work to this county, Johnny. The Industrial Estate in Rathmore and the eight hundred jobs that came with it didn't land here by accident, you know.

JOHNNY I know.

TESS The new harbour wall below in the village? The grants for the new trawlers tied up there? Where do you think they came from?

JOHNNY I know where they came from, Tess. But people have short memories. And whatever Brennan has in mind for Kilgallen a Community Park won't bring much in the way of jobs.

CONROY That's right, Johnny — it probably won't. 'What kind of country?' Isn't that what you said we were playing for, Katherine? Looks like the game is on.

KATHERINE Not tonight it isn't! Now, I propose a toast! (*Raises glass*) To our new Minister! To battles won and the battle to come! And to a country we can all be proud to live in!

The double doors open. STEPHEN *enters. Silence.*

Stephen. Are you okay?

STEPHEN I've been better. Congratulations, Minister — I heard the news on the radio. (*Pause*) Only good news there's going to be around here today, I'm afraid.

TESS What is it, Stephen?

STEPHEN Laura is dead, Tess.

Silence.

CONROY When?

STEPHEN An hour ago. Two hours. Does it matter?

JOE I'm very sorry, Stephen.

STEPHEN (*Looking at* KATHERINE) We all are.

KATHERINE May God have mercy on her soul.

CONROY May God have mercy on all of us.

TESS Were you with her?

STEPHEN I sure was, Tess. Holding her snow-white hand all the way to the crossing gates. (*Pours champagne*) Starlight now, Johnny. That's what they become. That's where the good souls go. And Laura sure qualified on that score, didn't she?

He raises glass. No one responds.

CONROY (*Looking to* KATHERINE) We should have been there.

STEPHEN It wouldn't have made any difference. Laura never came round. She had all the company she needed.

Silence.

KATHERINE Have the Guards been told?

STEPHEN Sergeant Coogan called to express his sympathy. And, in that time-honoured phrase, invited me to accompany him to the Station.

TESS Ma said you gave them a statement on the night of the accident.

STEPHEN That's right, Tess, I did. (*Looking at* KATHERINE) But she didn't tell you what it said, did she?

JOHNNY What *did* it say?

STEPHEN That I ran away. Left the scene, as they say.

TESS To get help?

STEPHEN I passed half a dozen houses on the Sky Road. Every one of them had a phone.

TESS Where did you go?

STEPHEN It was two in the morning. The bar was closed. I went back there.

JOHNNY And did what?

STEPHEN What I do best, Johnny. I waited.

KATHERINE Your brother was in shock. Anyone of us might have done the same.

JOHNNY I don't believe this. What did you do, Stephen? Have a beer? Play the bloody jukebox?!

KATHERINE He telephoned here and told us what happened. I called an ambulance as soon as we heard. Laura was in a coma when they found her. The Guards picked Stephen up in the pub. Is there anything else you need to know, Johnny?

TESS (*To* CONROY) Why didn't you tell us?

KATHERINE We were trying to protect our son. Is that a crime, Tess?

TESS No. But leaving the scene of an accident is.

CONROY What did Sergeant Coogan have to say?

STEPHEN Nothing's going to happen in a hurry. They'll send a file to the DPP and take it from there.

Silence.

JOE I should go. I'll see you later, Tess.

KATHERINE (*As* JOE *goes*) Joe? (*He stops*) Can you keep this out of the papers?

JOE   Not if there's a charge. (*To* CONROY) Stephen's a Minister's son now, Frank. If they can't stick something on you they'll go for the next best thing.

      JOE *exits.*

KATHERINE   (*To* CONROY) We'd better be going, too.

CONROY   Going where?

KATHERINE   To the rally.

CONROY   Cancel it.

KATHERINE   I'm afraid that won't be possible.

CONROY   It will if I'm not there. Now are you going to go into the house and get on that phone or do I have to do it myself?

KATHERINE   It's not that simple.

CONROY   Laura is *dead*, Katherine!

KATHERINE   Yes. And we'll mourn her in our own time. But that does not relieve us of our responsibilities.

TESS   To what?

KATHERINE   There were three thousand people in the Square when you left. In an hour's time that number will have doubled. What do you propose we tell them, Frank?

TESS   Tell them to go to hell. They don't own him, do they?

KATHERINE   No. But they put him where he got to today. And now they want a little bit of us back in return. That's our contract. Even if the timing is unfortunate.

JOHNNY   (*To* CONROY) Ma is right. If you don't go they'll think we're hiding.

TESS   Or maybe they'll think you've got your priorities right.

JOHNNY   Da has nothing to prove on that score. You should remember who's responsible for the mess we're in, Tess.

TESS   And you should remember that Stephen is still your brother.

KATHERINE   (*To* CONROY) There'll be a minute's silence for

Laura before your speech. I'll cancel the afters at the hotel — the band and parade as well. (*Pause*) You're not the only one with tears to shed, Frank. But we'll not shed them tonight.

KATHERINE *exits.* JOHNNY *unsure what to do.*

CONROY (*Looking at* TESS) Go with your mother, Johnny. I'll see you later.

JOHNNY *looks at* STEPHEN. *Exits.*

I'm sorry, Stephen.

STEPHEN So am I. But none of that's going to bring Laura back to the land of the living. Why don't you and Tess go get yourselves ready?

TESS (*Looking at* CONROY) I'm not going anywhere.

CONROY (*Ignoring this*) We'll need to make arrangements for a funeral. Give the convent a call, Tess. Tell them we'll handle everything.

TESS That's what we do best, isn't it?

CONROY (*To* STEPHEN) You'll need a solicitor, Stephen. We'll meet James Patterson first thing in the morning and agree our best options.

STEPHEN Do I get a choice?

CONROY I'm trying to help.

STEPHEN Yeah? Well, you could start by wising up. It's going to take more than Jimmy Patterson to get me out of this hole. Not to mention bringing Laura back from her new home in the starry skies. Never yet met a solicitor could pull that one off.

CONROY I have to go. (*Beat*) Superintendent Ryan will be at the rally. I'll have a word with him.

STEPHEN No.

CONROY I just want to get the lie of the land.

STEPHEN The 'lie of the land' is I've just been cautioned and you're a Government Minister. Add one to the other and see what you get.

CONROY You're not a bloody criminal.

STEPHEN Not yet.

CONROY Please, Stephen.

STEPHEN I said no. You never did that for anyone, remember.

CONROY This is different.

STEPHEN No it's not. It's what you staked a career on.

CONROY You're my son, Stephen.

STEPHEN And I'll take what's coming.

TESS (*As* CONROY *begins to leave*) You don't have to go, Da.

CONROY Your mother is right. We have a contract. (*To* STEPHEN) I'll see you later.

CONROY *exits. Silence.* STEPHEN *pours another drink.*

STEPHEN You want some?

TESS No.

STEPHEN Hardly the drink for the occasion, is it? You should go with them, Tess.

TESS I don't want to go with them. I want to stay here with you.

STEPHEN (*Pause*) I always figured she'd make her way back. Knew a guy once took the big sleep for fourteen weeks straight, then woke up and asked for his breakfast. I was kind of hoping Laura might do the same.

TESS It was an accident, Stephen. There's no one to blame.

STEPHEN Except I ran away, didn't I?

TESS You panicked. It happens.

STEPHEN So I hear. Understandably, however, the Guardians of the Peace are taking a slightly less cheery view of my little midnight run.

TESS Why didn't you tell me?

STEPHEN It's not the sort of thing you go bragging about, is it?

TESS You're not on your own, Stephen. You make sure you remember that.

STEPHEN I will.

TESS Maybe you *should* let him speak to the Guards.

STEPHEN No.

TESS You're not in a position to be choosy.

STEPHEN Our new Minister is not in a position to compromise himself.

TESS Nobody need know.

STEPHEN *He'd* know. You forget, Tess. It's not just idle rhetoric. The bugger actually *does* think he can change the world — or at least that ulcerated little corner known as the Irish body politic. I'm damned if I'd let him do anything to compromise that.

TESS Even if it means going to prison?

STEPHEN (*Smiles*) You can go character witness for me.

TESS Families don't count.

STEPHEN Just as well.

TESS You can count on me, Stephen.

STEPHEN Just like Laura thought she could count on us. (*Crosses to telescope*) First night she set foot here she looked through this telescope. I showed her old Jupiter, the King of the Planets. Pointed out the Galilean moons to impress her. *Io, Europa, Ganymede* and *Callisto*. And she sure was bitten. Looked at me afterwards like I was some kind of conjurer, like I'd just opened the gates of heaven and let her have a peep. (*As he opens the telescope*) The following night she wanted to see them again but everything had changed. I forgot to tell her that nothing was constant, that the moons changed position from night to night. I thought that was the attraction; everything shifting, nothing ever staying the same. But I could tell Laura was disappointed. I think after all those years in that convent some sort of certainty was what she was counting on from us. I think that's what she thought she'd found here. (*Pause*) I guess it wasn't to be, was it, Tess?

As lights fade and the scene ends we hear audio recording from the Apollo 11 *moon landing. The recording continues in the crossfade to Scene Two.*

Scene Two

Two hours later. As lights come up the Apollo *audio recording is fading and we see* STEPHEN *alone on stage, looking through the lens of the telescope.*

STEPHEN *Mare Cognitum, Mare Vaporum, Mare Serenitatis —*

> JOE *enters. He watches as* STEPHEN *continues to look through the telescope, savouring the sound of every word.*

Mare Nectaris, Mare Tranquillitatis.

> JOE *clears his throat to announce his presence.*

Litania Lunaris, Joseph! The Litany of the Moon. A sort of mantra in troubled times. Never fails to do the trick, either. You want to try?

JOE My comforts are a little more earthbound, Stephen.

STEPHEN We'll take it where we find it, eh?

JOE Is Tess about?

STEPHEN I believe she had a rendezvous with an undertaker. (*Pause*) July 20th, 1969! Ring a bell, Joe?

JOE Should it?

STEPHEN (*American accent*) *'One small step for man. One giant leap for mankind.'* The Armstrong and Aldrin Show! Greatest day in the history of space flight, Joe. But a question for you. Who was the third?

JOE Third what?

STEPHEN Astronaut. Voyager of the Stars!

JOE You got me.

STEPHEN Gets everybody. Mike Collins, that's who. No one remembers him, Joe. And why? Because he wasn't there. Not where the action was, anyway. Not dunking his little piggy toes onto the moon like his buddies got to do, but circling around in the wild black yonder minding the shop. Somebody's got to do it, I suppose. Otherwise, how the hell are they going to get home? I guess he just drew the short straw.

JOE Does this little yarn have a point, Stevie?

STEPHEN It sure does. From the moment old Buzz and Neil went shootin' off to the moon for their rendezvous with history, Mike Collins was on his own. And I mean on his own. Twenty-six hours, Joe. Thirteen revolutions of Old Mr Green Cheese, two hours for every orbit, just those flickering little dials keeping a static-filled line to the folks back down in Houston. Who, if the truth were known, weren't too exercised about Mike right then, the real theatre being elsewhere. But here's the rub, Joe. For forty-eight minutes in every two-hour slingshot Mike Collins flew his ship round the far side of the moon and, in so doing, acquired the state of Loss of Signal. *Loss of Signal*, Joe, that's the point. Radio contact terminated, normal service resumed as soon as possible but, in the meantime, goodnight Mike and God bless. That's duty for you, Joe, that's service in the greater good. But can you imagine the prize? See, I don't think Mike Collins drew the short straw at all. I think he was the lucky one. Forty-eight minutes out there in the gloaming, forty-eight minutes out of reach. Unshackled, Joe. Beyond pity or hope, beyond blame or blessing. And so quiet you can hear, not just your heartbeat, but the blood coursing through the chambers of your heart. Just you and the stars of heaven. Down to bare metal, then, Joe, down to the only questions that really matter. Between you and you.

Silence.

JOE Sounds like you envy him the trip.

STEPHEN Wouldn't you? (*Pause*) Right now I just can't figure out why he ever came home.

31

JOE   You spend too much time looking through that yoke, y'know.

STEPHEN   They probably said the same to Galileo. Blame it on the Minister. Bought me a telescope the day he was first elected to the Dáil. 'Stars for a star!' he said. 'Stars for my brightest star!' (*The memory hurts. He drinks the remains of a glass of champagne*) Not how it turned out though, was it?

JOE   That sounds suspiciously like self-pity.

STEPHEN   (*Smiles*) Yes, it does, doesn't it? So — What news from Rathmore?

JOE   You know your father. He spoke from the heart.

STEPHEN   Bravo!

JOE   It can't have been easy, Stephen — on any of them.

STEPHEN   I know. Now you mustn't let me detain you. If Tess shows up I'll tell her you called.

JOE   As a matter of fact I was looking for you.

STEPHEN   I've been busy.

JOE   You've been hiding.

STEPHEN   No. Loss of signal, that's all.

JOE   I'm on your side, Stephen.

STEPHEN   Then leave me alone. Some other time, Joe.

JOE   Laura died today, not you. Cutting off me and your family is not the smartest way to deal with that.

STEPHEN   No? Sure feels like it.

JOE   You're not the only one who's suffering.

STEPHEN   I'll be the only one doing time.

JOE   *You* crashed the car, Stephen. *You* ran away.

Silence.

STEPHEN   Touché!

JOE   I'm sorry. (*Pause*) I called by the Garda Station on my way from Rathmore.

STEPHEN   Oh yeah?

JOE   I have a few pals there — Goes with the job, I suppose. They told me your blood sample was positive.

STEPHEN And science never lies, does it? As a matter of fact I hadn't been drinking. Not until I legged it back to the pub. But I would say that, wouldn't I?

JOE For what it's worth, I believe you. (*Beat*) What's the story, Stephen?

STEPHEN How d'you mean?

JOE You know what I mean. We've been friends since I came to this town. I'm just curious how I missed this.

STEPHEN Missed what?

JOE I'm trying to understand how Laura is lying on a mortuary slab and my best friend is looking at a jail sentence.

STEPHEN Why don't you go back to your 'pals' and get a look at my statement. It's all in black and white.

JOE Only what you told them. I already did, Stephen, and it doesn't add up.

STEPHEN Which part?

JOE Pretty much all of it. You lock up the pub, saunter up to the house here and whip the keys of your Da's car. Then you cruise by Laura's flat and invite her to go for a moonlight drive.

STEPHEN That's what happened.

JOE Except it's two o'clock in the morning.

STEPHEN I was always a creature of impulse.

JOE I'll grant you that. Where d'you go, Stephen? Stargazing?

STEPHEN Yeah. Laura liked to look at the stars. Maybe I liked to show them off. It wasn't the first time.

JOE First time since she left here and got a place of her own. That was two years ago, Stephen. What was it? You suddenly fancy a midnight trip down memory lane?

STEPHEN Yeah, maybe I did. Maybe that's what it was. Or maybe it's what you and everybody else think it was. That I was screwing her. Is that what you want me to tell you? That I shagged her out on Silver Strand, then rammed the Minister's car into a tree and left her for dead?

JOE   That's not what I think.

STEPHEN   I don't care what you think. 'What's the story, Stephen?' The story is she's dead.

JOE   And you're *not*. That's why it matters what you were up to that night.

STEPHEN   It doesn't matter *now*.

JOE   Listen to me, Stephen.

STEPHEN   Go home, Joe.

JOE   Listen to me. Please! You're my best mate. I won't keep watching you give your life away.

STEPHEN   You're crossing the line, Joe.

JOE   Not before time maybe. You've been standing the other side of that line for years.

STEPHEN   Is that so?

JOE   Yeah it is. And I know why. But then one day Laura came along. And that line shifted when she showed up here. I know you weren't screwing her. But I know what she meant to you. And you know what? No matter how hard I try, I can't see you running down that road and leaving her behind.

STEPHEN   I'm having just a little trouble with that one myself, Joe. But that's what happened. That's what I did.

TESS *enters.*

Just in time, Tess. Your fiancé here's been giving me the third degree.

TESS   Why not? Everyone else has had a go.

JOE   I was trying to help.

TESS   I'm surprised you were able to drag yourself away from the festivities.

JOE   You know I had to go. I was doing my job.

TESS   Of course. Story of the night, it seems. (*Picks up champagne bottle*) Who polished off the bubbly?

STEPHEN   It was going flat.

TESS   A bit like the evening. But it's not over yet. (*Takes remains of another glass*)

JOE   Maybe you've had enough, Tess.

TESS Blame it on our esteemed local undertaker. Francis Xavier O'Gorman 'sorry for your troubles' me into his office to make 'the arrangements'. Two glasses of pretty memorable port wine later we'd only gotten to the Removal. By the third glass gamey old Francis was trying to remove something else but that's another story! Duly fortified, I set off on a trip through night-town Seafield. All four pubs, if you must know. Well, three acutally, our own being closed in deference to the night that's in it. (*To* JOE) Purpose of tour? Taking soundings, as the Da would say! (*Pause*) And, by Christ, the message was loud and clear. Not that anybody said much, but silence talks, doesn't it, Joe? All they were short of was a hanging rope.

STEPHEN What did you expect, Tess?

TESS An ounce of compassion might have been a start.

JOE Don't be so bloody naive. This isn't a soap opera, Tess. If Stephen wasn't your brother you'd feel exactly like they do — and with good reason.

TESS Meaning what?

JOE Meaning there's a woman lying on a mortuary stone below in that hospital and maybe she wouldn't be there if your brother had done things differently. And if you think it's bad now, Tess, you'd better brace yourself. (*Beat*) Stephen's blood test has come back. They'll be adding a drink driving charge to the list. Try that for a test of compassion.

Silence.

TESS I won't judge my brother.

JOE You won't have to.

JOHNNY *enters.*

STEPHEN Hello, Johnny. (*Telescope*) Want a look?

JOHNNY No.

STEPHEN *Pleiades* is high in the northern sky. It'll be gone in a few days.

JOHNNY I said no.

STEPHEN Johnny was apprentice astronomer to the court of Conroy, Joe. Taught him the name and position of every constellation in the northern sky. That right, Johnny?

JOHNNY I don't remember.

STEPHEN Course you do. *Perseus, Auriga, Cassiopeia, Orion —*

JOHNNY I said I don't remember!

Silence.

JOE It was a good night, Johnny.

JOHNNY Yeah. All things considered.

JOE Old guy at the door of Power's Bar said the last man to pack the Square like that was Éamon de Valera.

JOHNNY So I hear.

JOE He said the only thing Frank Conroy doesn't do is walk on water.

JOHNNY I'm sure he would if he had to.

JOE Aye. (*Pause*) Are your folks back?

JOHNNY I took a lift from Sam Dowling. (*Pause*) He dropped me at the hospital. I wanted to see Laura but they wouldn't let me.

TESS It's late, Johnny. I'll go round there with you in the morning.

JOHNNY I wanted to see her tonight. I just wanted to say goodbye, that's all.

JOE Leave it now, Johnny.

JOHNNY No. No, I won't leave it. You didn't know her, Joe. All you ever saw was the woman who ran my father's office. You don't remember the girl that walked up our avenue six years ago, a cardboard suitcase carrying everything she owned. I remember that. And so does he. He remembers because he took care of her.

STEPHEN We all did, Johnny.

JOHNNY   You don't know anything anymore so you just shut up and listen. (*To* JOE) We couldn't get two words out of her when she came here first. To tell the truth I wasn't too pushed but Stevie here was different. Maybe he was just curious or maybe he just felt sorry for her but he kept working on her. She came round, too. Took a while, but she did. And Jesus, Joe, when she started talkin' she couldn't stop. It was like she'd been savin' up all her life for the time someone'd listen to her. (*Beat*) And she said it was all down to him. Said he was the big brother she never had. She said he taught her how to dream.

STEPHEN   Johnny.

JOHNNY   No. You listen.

STEPHEN   Can't listen.

JOHNNY   Why's that? Did you remember her dreams when you went running down the Sky Road that night?

STEPHEN   No.

JOHNNY   What *did* you remember?

TESS   That's enough.

JOHNNY   No! Laura felt safe here, Tess. Seventeen years a frightened rabbit beyond in that convent. And then she found a home. She trusted us. She trusted *him*. And now she's lying in that morgue and I can't even say goodbye. (*To* STEPHEN) I want you to tell me how my big brother could let that happen.

STEPHEN   I don't know how, Johnny.

JOHNNY   I looked up to you. Just like she did. Oddball for sure, crazy as they come, but I loved you for that. I would have gone to hell and back just to sit at your feet and listen to you talking about that sky. (*Pause*) I just want you to know it's different now.

STEPHEN   I know, Johnny.

JOHNNY   (*To* TESS) I'm going inside. A few of the local Cumann are on their way back here for supper. He shouldn't be here when they arrive.

TESS   Stephen's not going anywhere.

JOHNNY   (*To* STEPHEN) I'm asking you to leave.

37

TESS   And I'm telling you he's not going anywhere! There was an accident. A terrible accident. Laura is dead but Stephen is still your brother. There's people not fit to lace his shoes queuing up to judge and condemn him tonight. But you won't do it here. Because that's your brother you're looking at and you'll be loyal to him now whether you like it or not.

JOHNNY   My loyalty is to this family.

TESS   *This family*! Who do you think we are, Johnny? The Kennedys?

JOHNNY   No. The Conroys. That name still means something to me.

TESS   I know what it means, too. I travelled every mile of this county for the last six months because I believe in my father and I believe in our name. But if it's worth anything it'll survive the moral superiority of the peasants I met down in that village tonight. Not to mention yours.

JOHNNY   You don't get it, do you? You make it sound like we're some kind of broken toy that just needs glue. My father stood in front of six thousand people tonight and all he felt was shame. That's what's broken, Tess. We'll bury Laura and then we'll pick up the pieces as best we can. But not with him. Not me, anyway.

We hear the sound of cars approaching.

STEPHEN   Relax, Johnny. I'll go.

TESS   No.

STEPHEN   It's alright, Tess. You go put on your party hat, Johnny — I'll leave by the back door.

JOHNNY *exits.*

JOE   (*To* TESS) Maybe it's time we were leaving too.

TESS   I'm staying here tonight.

JOE   That might not be such a good idea.

TESS   I'm staying *here*, Joe.

JOE   (*Pause*) Whatever you think. (*Pause*) There was something else I learnt tonight, Stephen.

STEPHEN   I get the feeling you're about to pass it on.

JOE   For what it's worth. Though I'm not sure it will come as news.

STEPHEN   I'm intrigued!

JOE   The oul' fella I was talking to in Rathmore. He used to canvass for your grandfather in the old days and by all accounts still does the same for your father. He said Frank had been due out west for a Clinic the night of the car crash. It was the day he'd done the deal with Grogan in Dublin and no one expected him to show. He did, though. By the time he turned up his clients had all gone but, typical of Frank, he insisted the old guy take him round to the houses of the people he'd missed. The business of the night concluded, he stood drinks in a roadside bar for a few of the local Cumann. It was near closing time when he left.

TESS   What's the point, Joe?

JOE   The point is Laura was with him.

TESS   So? Laura did all his Clinics. You know that.

JOE   I didn't know she was with him that night.

TESS   And now you do.

JOE   That's right. Now I do. Your father was drinking, Tess. The guy I met in Rathmore wasn't making anything of it — just a couple of beers for the night was in it, he said. But it might have been enough to put a soon-to-be Government Minister over the limit.

TESS   What are you trying to suggest?

JOE   I'm not suggesting anything. Am I, Stephen?

STEPHEN   No. You're not.

TESS   That's not what it bloody well sounds like. If you have something to say, then spit it out, Joe.

JOE   I think I've said enough.

STEPHEN   I think so, too.

TESS   Nobody's going anywhere until my so-called

fiancé finishes what he started.

JOE   Maybe your father might be better qualified to do that.

TESS   Yeah? Then if you're such a fearless investigator why don't you go inside and ask him?

JOE   Because I'm not sure I want to know the answer. Do you, Tess?

TESS   I don't believe this! I don't believe what's coming out of your mouth, Joe. Don't you think we've suffered enough?

JOE   I think Stephen has.

TESS   You bastard! I thought I knew you. I thought you knew my father.

JOE   I'm sorry.

TESS   So am I.

STEPHEN   Joe doesn't mean any harm, Tess — he's just clutching at straws, that's all. And we won't hold that against him, will we? You ask my father what you like, Joe — but I can save you the bother. I know Laura was with him earlier that night because she told me. And he *did* have a few drinks — but he didn't drive home. Laura did. She's not around anymore to tell you that herself, but she did tell me so you're going to have to take my word for it. Just like you, Joe, I'd like the story of the rest of that night to be different — but it's not and it's not going to be. (*Pause*) Goodnight, Tess.

TESS   Don't go. Please.

STEPHEN   I'm going home.

TESS   This is your home.

STEPHEN   You know where I live.

JOE   She knows where you hide, Stephen. Every night for seven years now. She knows what you do when you lock up the bar and turn down the lights. She knows the place on the counter in front of the clock. The whiskey gradually kicking in, the reel beginning to roll.

STEPHEN   I don't know what you're talking about.

JOE   I'm talking about your daughter. I'm talking about

how you died the night Cassie did. They might as well have buried you with her.

STEPHEN Don't, Joe.

JOE Am I wrong, Tess? How many nights did you sit at that counter with him before you knew even you couldn't bring him back?

TESS Why are you doing this?

JOE Because that's what Stephen does. That's all he's done for seven years. Just runs that movie over and over in his head, hoping somehow the end will be different next time. That's what you do, Stephen. And you know what? I think that's what you were doing the night of the car crash.

STEPHEN No. Picture House closed that night.

JOE It never closes. Because the end is never different. Cassie got sick and then she died and it was the one thing on God's green earth you couldn't protect her from. You blamed yourself, Stephen, and no matter what anyone tried to tell you you never stopped doing that. That's why Cassie's mother left you. It's why Johnny is heir to the Conroy dynasty. And that's why going to prison wouldn't bother you too much. You don't have anything left to lose, do you?

CONROY *enters.*

CONROY It's cold out here. Why don't you come inside?

STEPHEN Good of you to ask, Da. But I wouldn't want to spoil the party.

CONROY There's no party. It's just a few friends come to pay their respects.

TESS Did you have a good night?

CONROY No. You were right. We should never have gone ahead with it.

TESS It doesn't matter now.

JOE I'll see you tomorrow, Tess.

TESS *does not reply.* JOE *leaves.*

CONROY   Are you not going with Joe?

TESS   No.

CONROY   Your mother's inside — she could do with a hand.

TESS   (*Pause*) Goodnight, Stephen.

TESS *exits.*

CONROY   There's nothing quite so piercing, is there?

STEPHEN   As what?

CONROY   The accusing eyes of a disappointed child.

STEPHEN   She'll get over it. (*Begins to leave*) Give my regards to the foot soldiers.

CONROY   We need to talk, Stephen.

STEPHEN   Hardly the time or place, is it? We'll talk tomorrow.

CONROY   What I have to say won't wait until tomorrow. (*Pause*) I spoke to Superintendent Ryan at the rally tonight.

STEPHEN   I told you that's dangerous ground.

CONROY   We're hardly in a position to choose our ground. I didn't know you'd been drinking on the night of the accident.

STEPHEN   A small fly in the ointment right enough.

CONROY   It might have been helpful if I'd known before I met Ryan.

STEPHEN   It might have been helpful if none of this had happened either. I told you already — I'll take what's coming.

CONROY   What's coming is a prison sentence.

STEPHEN   I didn't expect a St Christopher medal.

CONROY   Ryan has agreed to meet us here tomorrow. We need to sort this out, Stephen.

STEPHEN   That's Taoiseach Grogan's language, Da. What's this you used to call him? Mr Fix-it, wasn't it? You try and fix this and you betray everything you've ever believed in.

CONROY   It seems to me I've done that already.

STEPHEN   Now you listen to me, Minister. You didn't ask for this. It was *fait accompli*. (*Pause*) A car, an accident and a critically injured passenger. But you didn't write the next scene. I did. All on my own.

CONROY Your mother and I allowed you to. *I* allowed you to.

STEPHEN I didn't ask permission.

CONROY Can't we at least tell the truth to each other? *I* ran away, Stephen. Laura was dying and I ran away.

STEPHEN You came back here. You would have called the Guards if Ma hadn't called me first. The rest was out of your hands. Ma's hands too, just so you're clear. This was my idea and I'll see it through.

CONROY No. I let you do what you did because I was a coward. And a bloody hypocrite, to boot. The very day of the accident I sat in Emmet Grogan's office and, with all the moral righteousness I could muster, told him I didn't want power at any price. Grogan laughed at me. Told me I was a fool, said there was no price he wouldn't pay for it. I despised him for that. Yet just a few hours later I ran the length of the Sky Road to save my political skin. The only difference between Grogan and me is that he was honest enough to admit *his* craving.

STEPHEN Great speech. You know what the moral of the story is: you're not perfect!

CONROY No, Stephen. People in glasshouses. That's the moral. (*Pause*) We'll meet Ryan in the morning. Not to fix anything but to tell the truth and face the consequences.

STEPHEN The truth is a moveable feast.

CONROY Who's using Grogan's language now?

STEPHEN Maybe I've learnt something from the old fox. Consequences are a different matter, though. Consequences are something our gallant leader is seldom troubled by. But you will be if you go spilling the beans now.

CONROY This has cost enough already. I can't bring Laura back, but I won't sacrifice my son for a seat in Government.

STEPHEN You already have. And you know why. It's called the greater good.

CONROY No good can come from lies.

STEPHEN Now there's moral absolutism, if ever I heard it. We were talking about consequences. Well, here's another absolute: you ride into town tomorrow on the white horse of your conscience and there's just two kinds of people left in this country — winners and losers. The winners are Emmet Grogan and all the other Grogans who run this little green isle like it was their private club. Every crooked councillor who ever took the contents of an envelope, all the two-bit shysters who buy off politicians like sweets from a corner store. They're the winners, Da — and, boy, will they have something to celebrate. The losers are the rest of us. The men and women inside that door who gave their lives to what your Party once stood for, who'd give their lives for you because of what you still stand for. And the biggest losers, Da: the thousands you'll never know, the people Grogan and his kind trample on, who trust you to make a difference. Not just to a rotten political system, but to their lives. Now that's as close to a party political broadcast as I'm ever likely to get, but I hope you get the message. Winners and losers, Da. You decide.

CONROY You lose either way.

STEPHEN Maybe not.

CONROY You'll go to prison, Stephen.

STEPHEN There's worse places.

CONROY No. That's a bridge too far. I should pay for this.

STEPHEN You will. You'll carry it with you for the rest of your life. But we're going to be the only ones who'll know.

CONROY I can't do this to you.

STEPHEN Then do it *for* me. Please.

CONROY I won't let you sacrifice your life to protect a coward.

STEPHEN It's not a sacrifice. And you're no coward. I *want* to do this.

CONROY Why?

STEPHEN   Because you're my father and I'm your son. May-
           be it's no more complicated than that. I couldn't
           stand in your shoes. Not the way you stood in your
           old man's. Circumstances, as they say, beyond our
           control. I'm your dark star, Da — always will be.
           But this is my contribution to the dynasty. See, I
           believe in you, too — just like all the others.

CONROY   What's there to believe in? Look at me and tell
           me what you believe in now. I'm a hollow man,
           Stephen.

STEPHEN   You're my father. That's enough for me.

           KATHERINE *enters.*

KATHERINE You're an ungracious host, Minister — Blaise Power
           is listing on the couch. You'd better go in before he
           capsizes.

CONROY   Get rid of them, Katherine.

KATHERINE They've come to pay their respects.

CONROY   Tell them I'll see them tomorrow.

KATHERINE You're in Dublin tomorrow. First day in your new
           Department!

CONROY   There's not going to *be* any new Department.

KATHERINE You're tired, Frank. Give them twenty minutes
           and I'll see them off.

CONROY   Did you not hear what I said?

KATHERINE Every word. And you heard what I said. It's been
           a long day — for all of us. We'll talk in the morn-
           ing before you go to Dublin.

CONROY   I'm not going to Dublin! We've made a terrible
           mistake, Katherine. I should never have let it come
           to this. But it's not going any further.

KATHERINE Do you have the slightest idea what you're talking
           about?

CONROY   I would have thought it was perfectly clear. I
           intend to tell the Guards the truth and resign from
           Government.

KATHERINE (*Hard anger*) I'm talking about the consequences!

CONROY   I'm aware of the consequences.

KATHERINE A pity you didn't give some thought to them three weeks ago when you came crying down the Sky Road.

CONROY I know. I'll regret that to my dying day. I'll regret everything that followed, Katherine, but it's time to tell the truth.

KATHERINE And wash thirty-six years of your life down the drain?

CONROY I already have.

KATHERINE No. You haven't. And you're not going to. That's why we did this. You think my conscience is clear? You don't have the copyright on regret, Frank. But I know why I did what I did.

CONROY To save your husband's glittering career.

KATHERINE Don't patronize me! And don't flatter yourself. I don't give tuppence for your career. No more than you ever did. I didn't marry the State car parked in that drive. I fell in love with a man who was so preposterously naive as to believe that public service was not a passport to private gain but a privilege and a responsibility to be treasured and respected. Fool that you are, you've been faithful to that belief all your life, Frank. As far as I'm concerned that scale of naivety is worth protecting. Laura Gavin's death hasn't changed my mind.

CONROY And if your son goes to prison?

STEPHEN That's my choice.

CONROY I'm not giving you that choice.

KATHERINE You no longer have it to give. I understand the legal term is conspiracy to cause a miscarriage of justice. You bare your soul to the nation in the morning and Stephen and I are implicated with you. I'd hasten slowly if I were you.

The verandah doors open. TESS *stands there.*

TESS The troops are getting restless.

Silence. KATHERINE *and* STEPHEN *watch* CONROY.

CONROY *looks at each of them in turn.*

Is there something I should know? (*Pause*) I asked a question.

KATHERINE Nothing at all, Tess. The Minister was just taking the air. We're going in now.

> *Pause.* CONROY *goes back into the house.* KATHERINE *looks at* STEPHEN *before following* CONROY *in.* TESS *watches* STEPHEN *who returns her stare.* TESS *goes back in.* STEPHEN *crosses to the telescope and looks through the lens in a reprise of the beginning of the scene.*

STEPHEN *Mare Crisium, Mare Fecunditatis, Mare Undarum.*

> *And continues as light fades to black.*

> *Fra Mauro, Mare Kepler, Mare Galileo, Sinus Iridum, Sinus Roris, Lacus Mortis.*

ACT TWO

Same scene. A winter night, four years later. The 'Welcome Home' sign and bunting have gone but little else has changed in the years that have passed. As lights come up on the empty space we hear the following:

VOICE OVER Good morning, and here is the News. The Minister for the Environment, Frank Conroy, has resigned and put down a leadership challenge to the Taoiseach, Emmet Grogan. In a shock announcement last night Mr Conroy, who has been in office for four years, said he had tendered his resignation following the rejection by the Taoiseach of his proposal to sack and replace the members of the Anti-Corruption Commission. The Commission was appointed by the Taoiseach almost two years after a post-election deal with Mr Conroy. In his resignation statement Mr Conroy said the Commission, as presently constituted, was widely regarded as ineffectual and pledged that, if elected Taoiseach, a new Commission would be given the power to carry out its work in the manner he had always intended. In a follow-up statement released by the Taoiseach's office last night Mr Grogan said he had every trust in the integrity of the current Anti-Corruption Commission. The Taoiseach said he looked forward to meeting Mr Conroy's challenge head-on.

STEPHEN *enters, carrying a ghetto blaster in one hand and a pair of binoculars in the other and with a picnic blanket draped around his shoulders. He is singing the Victorian love song, 'Sweet Genevieve',*

48

and is in very obvious good spirits. He unfolds the
trestle table which, along with some folded garden
chairs, lies along the wall of the house. He places the
ghetto blaster on the table and turns it on. We hear
something from Nat King Cole. STEPHEN *joins in the*
song as he brings one of the garden chairs downstage
and drapes the rug on it. He takes the binoculars and
begins to scan the night sky. After a moment or two
TESS *emerges from the house.*

STEPHEN Tessalonika! How the hell are ye?

TESS Hanging in. I don't need to ask how you're doing.

STEPHEN My cup runneth over, Tess. If I was any better I'd
have to go back to bed.

TESS What are you up to?

STEPHEN All will be revealed! (*Turns off ghetto blaster*) More
to the point, what are *you* up to? The gig must be
only warming up by now.

TESS All that fervour was a little more than I could
handle.

STEPHEN We can but imagine! Has the old man been canon-
ized yet?

TESS Just a matter of time. It's quite a shindig.

STEPHEN Forty years of public service to town and country!
That's reason enough for a hooley, I suppose.

TESS That why you didn't go?

STEPHEN Prior engagement. I was there in spirit.

TESS More than I can say.

STEPHEN You showed up, Tess — the prodigal daughter has
returned!

TESS For three days. I'm going back to London in the
morning.

STEPHEN Three days, three weeks — we are grateful, O Lord,
for these thy gifts! The Minister all but levitated
when he heard you were coming home.

TESS Is that why he's been avoiding me?

STEPHEN He's a busy man.

TESS So I hear. It's more like an election rally than an
anniversary gig in that hotel.

49

STEPHEN It *is* an election rally. The anniversary is just an
         excuse to gather the troops.

TESS For the great crusade on Grogan's citadel!

STEPHEN That's right. Shame you can't hang around, Tess.
         Another few days and you could be the proud
         daughter of the new Taoiseach.

TESS That's a part I'm not sure I could do justice to.

STEPHEN You'd cope.

TESS Will he?

STEPHEN How d'you mean?

TESS Watching him in that hotel tonight it didn't seem
      much like he was enjoying the prospect of power.

STEPHEN He'll acclimatize. How's Ma doing?

TESS Last I saw she was playing a blinder.

STEPHEN She always does.

TESS There must have been three hundred people in
      that room. She shook every hand, knew every one
      of them by their first name, top brass to the lowest
      functionary. Then sat smiling down at them all
      from the top table as if she hadn't a care in the
      world.

STEPHEN Who says she has?

TESS You tell me, Stephen.

STEPHEN Ma's fine, Tess. We all are.

TESS Speaking of happy families, I ran into Johnny
      below.

STEPHEN Councillor Conroy, if you don't mind! Sitting at
         the right hand of the father, no doubt.

TESS Working the room, actually.

STEPHEN What he does best! Da spends most of his time in
         Dublin on affairs of state. Johnny and Ma keep the
         home fires burning in his absence.

TESS The good and faithful servants. Is Johnny still
      flogging houses?

STEPHEN I haven't heard anything to the contrary.

TESS Do you ever see him?

STEPHEN No.

TESS The old sores are the sweetest.

STEPHEN Something like that.

TESS   I went out to Laura's grave earlier.

STEPHEN   You won't find Laura under the clay, Tess. The stars of heaven. That's where you'll find her.

TESS   It wasn't Laura I was looking for.

STEPHEN   (*Pause*) We don't talk about all that anymore. It's a closed chapter now. Has been for a long time.

TESS   Yeah? I met Joe Harrington in the hotel tonight. (STEPHEN *is clearly surprised*) That didn't feel much like a closed chapter.

STEPHEN   I haven't seen Joe in a long time. How's he doing?

TESS   We met, I froze, we parted. I haven't seen him since we split up, Stephen. But I guess that's part of the history you don't talk about either.

STEPHEN   I was very sorry to hear it, Tess. I would have called but —

TESS   You were serving a prison sentence at the time.

STEPHEN   That's right, I was.

TESS   For something Joe believes you didn't do.

STEPHEN   All that stuff is over now, Tess. You don't have to like what you see when you come home. You don't have to approve of any of it. But it works. There's rules that make it work. And not looking back is number one.

TESS   They're not my rules, Stephen.

STEPHEN   True. But when in Rome, as they say. (STEPHEN *has untangled a string of carnival lights. He picks it up, throwing one end to* TESS) Here, give us a hand with these.

TESS   This your contribution to the celebrations?

STEPHEN   Not exactly. No disrespect to the Minister but Stevie is following his own star tonight.

TESS   What's the occasion?

STEPHEN   Halley's Comet, that's what! Last seen in this neck of the woods way back in 1910. Lit up the night sky for a few golden months, then goodnight and God bless and, with a flick of its blazing tail, bowed to the gallery and departed stage left! Seems Mr Halley is a little less the showman this time round. I've been scanning that sky every night for nearly two months now and if he's up there he ain't showing his face. But *Nil desperandum*, Tess! Maximum potential visibility, November 27th — which just happens to be tonight. If my calculations are correct Old Halley should be passing under the *Pleiades* between the hours of eleven and midnight — with a forecast for clear skies! (*Gesturing to lights*) And this? A small flicker of light in honour of the occasion — a welcome home for our beloved galactic voyager! Now come on, we don't have much time.

> *He fetches stepladder, props the ladder up against the wall of the house and begins to hang the lights, with* TESS *in attendance at the foot of the ladder.*

TESS What's with the 'we'?

STEPHEN You don't want to miss this, Tess. Halley is diving south. A few days' time it's going to disappear from the northern sky, won't be back for seventy-six years. *This* is history in the making!

TESS Seems to be the week for it. (*Pause*) You've still got your head in the clouds, haven't you?

STEPHEN Way above the clouds. Out there in the stratosphere. That's where old Stevie makes his bed these days.

TESS You happy there?

STEPHEN Much more than that. Loss of Signal, that's what I found. (*Pause*) Seems to me it's a state you're familiar with yourself.

TESS I get by.

STEPHEN That's it, Tess. Getting by. The only game in town.

> *Silence.* JOE *enters.*

JOE Hello, Stephen.

STEPHEN Joseph Michael Harrington! (*He is clearly moved to see his friend*) Welcome back, Joe. It's been too long.

JOE Yeah, it has. (*To* TESS) Hello again.

TESS Hello.

JOE (*To* STEPHEN) How've you been?

STEPHEN You know me — silverside up!

JOE I'm glad to hear it. I'm sorry it's been so long.

STEPHEN (*A glance to* TESS) The heart's a curse, Joe — no need to explain.

JOE I was back once or twice. I called by the pub but the guy behind the bar said you'd sold up.

STEPHEN Public life never suited me.

JOE I heard you'd moved back here.

STEPHEN There's just me and Ma, now. Oh, and the Minister of course — whenever he finds the homeward trail.

JOE Which isn't too often, I gather.

STEPHEN Fighting the good fight, Joe! I trust you've been keeping an eye on him.

JOE Our paths cross now and then — Dublin's a village, too.

STEPHEN Tess tells me you're down for the hooley.

JOE That's right.

STEPHEN I wouldn't have thought a gig like that was worth more than a footnote in a paper like yours.

JOE Not normally, no. But with the leadership contest on Tuesday your old man could be Taoiseach before the end of next week. My editor knows I used to live here — he wants a colour piece for this Sunday's paper.

TESS And colourful I'm sure it will be.

JOE That depends on what I write.

STEPHEN (*A glance to* TESS) The nation awaits with bated breath! (*Looks at stopwatch*) Which reminds me. Halley's Comet comes to Seafield, Joe — ringside seats for the chosen few. (*As he goes*) Mulled wine on the way for the night is in it, Tess. Don't let Scobie here out of your sight, and if you see anything moving in that sky —

TESS You'll be the first to know.

STEPHEN *exits.*

JOE   Same old Stephen.

TESS   You reckon? He's a bit further down the line if you ask me. Some day he'll float out into space and it'll be the last we'll ever see of him.

JOE   (*Lightly*) You're hardly in a position to talk about disappearing acts.

TESS   That's true.

JOE   I didn't mean to put the run on you tonight.

TESS   Initial shock, that's all. It's good to see you, Joe.

JOE   You too. You still holed up in London?

TESS   For my sins. One bunch of snotty-nosed school-kids is the same as another, I suppose. (*Pause*) And speaking of kids, I believe congratulations are in order.

JOE   (*Taken aback*) It's a small world.

TESS   Blame my mother — I get all the gossip. A little boy, wasn't it?

JOE   Yeah. Quite the handful, too.

TESS   I can imagine.

JOE   How about you?

TESS   (*Smiles*) I'm saving myself for the right man.

JOE   I'm sure he'll turn up.

TESS   He did. But I let him go, didn't I?

JOE   Maybe you had a lucky escape.

TESS   I don't think so. (*Pause*) I'm glad you're doing so well.

JOE   It's a job.

TESS   I wasn't talking about your job. Though, I grant you, it's a long way from the *Rathmore Leader*.

JOE   I suppose so.

TESS   And more of a vocation than a job, from what I read.

JOE   I wouldn't go that far.

TESS   That's what it looks like. I see you've been on Emmet Grogan's trail.

JOE   I follow lots of trails. Most of Grogan's bring you down the same blind alley you started from. Your father knows that better than most. I guess that's why he's finally taking him on.

TESS D'you think he's going to make it?

JOE From what I saw in the hotel tonight I think he's got every chance.

TESS Is the Party rediscovering its lost conscience, then?

JOE The Party doesn't *have* a conscience — you know that. But it does have a General Election to fight next year and the country is getting a taste for your father's kind of politics. The Parliamentary Party will vote for whoever gives them the best shot at another term. (*Pause*) I hope he does make it, Tess.

TESS Then you'd better make sure your 'colour piece' doesn't have too much colour in it.

JOE How d'you mean?

TESS I read your column every week, Joe. That probably says a whole lot more about me than I'd like to admit, but for four years it's been as close as I get to you. And one thing I know is you don't 'do' colour pieces.

JOE I'm nothing if not flexible.

TESS You're nothing if not persistent.

JOE Don't you think it's a bit late for that?

TESS Emmet Grogan wouldn't think so. Is that why you're here, Joe? Is this your second chance?

JOE Stephen didn't get a second chance. I reported what happened as best I could at the time.

TESS You reported what you were asked to swallow and never could.

JOE We were through all that four years ago.

TESS We sure were. And paid the price.

JOE I didn't have proof, Tess — you know that.

TESS Would you have used it if you had?

JOE I didn't have it to use. Stephen was his own accuser, remember. And in the absence of any other witness, what I thought didn't matter. Your father was entitled to his good name, Tess. He still is.

TESS My brother was entitled to his life.

JOE You didn't seem to think so at the time.

TESS I've had four years to think of nothing else. There

was another witness, Joe. Frank Conroy had all the proof you needed, didn't he? And you would have gone after him if I hadn't stopped you. I betrayed Stephen to protect my father. And to do that I had to sacrifice you as well. I know you've made another life for yourself, Joe, and I wish you nothing but the best. I just want you to know I'm sorry.

JOE I'm hardly the one you should be apologising to.

STEPHEN *returns, carrying empty wine glasses. He stands at the open door and ushers* KATHERINE *in.*

STEPHEN Enter an asylum seeker! Come on out and join the gang, Ma.

KATHERINE We meet again, Joe. I gather you made an early exit, too.

JOE I'd have offered you a lift if I'd known you were leaving.

KATHERINE I didn't know I *was* leaving. You didn't stay long either, Tess.

TESS No.

STEPHEN (*Who is now running an extension lead to connect the lights*) The folly of youth, Ma! I hear it was a great night. Tess said you played a blinder.

KATHERINE To which you replied, no doubt, that I always do. (*Without a flicker of resentment*) I'm aware of my function, Joe, the mute but smiling consort.

JOE Personally, I thought you were the star of the show.

KATHERINE You're too kind. If I was you were certainly the surprise guest.

JOE A working visit, I'm afraid.

KATHERINE I thought as much. You were welcome, nonetheless. Though it seems Johnny wasn't exactly rolling out the red carpet.

JOE No.

TESS Did I miss something?

KATHERINE Joe had a little contretemps with your brother in the hotel bar after you left. Knowing Johnny, it's unlikely they were arguing about the weather.

JOE No, we weren't. (*Pause*) You're right, Tess. This article I'm doing for Sunday's paper. It *is* a bit more than a colour piece.

STEPHEN (*Beat*) Do tell, Joe.

JOE I'm doing a story on Kilgallen House.

STEPHEN The Community Park that never was!

JOE That's right. Just another one of Grogan's broken promises to his Minister.

TESS How d'you mean?

JOE Kilgallen went up for auction shortly after the Party took office. Just like he said he would Grogan sent the OPW down to bid for the place but capped them at a price you wouldn't buy a caravan for. Paddy Brennan was the only other bidder. Grogan had him tipped off, of course — he bought the place for a song.

TESS What's Kilgallen got to do with Johnny?

JOE Brennan let the house go to ruin. Three days ago the County Council declared it a dangerous building and issued Brennan with a demolition order — this time next week a small slice of our history will be razed to the ground. By extraordinary co-incidence, on Monday next, the Council votes on a motion to rezone the land from agricultural to residential. Brennan stands to make a lot of money if the vote is passed.

STEPHEN That's hardly news. Every two-bit Council in the country has a few skeletons like that in its cupboard.

TESS But not every Council has a Minister's son sitting on it. Am I getting your drift, Joe?

JOE (*To* TESS) The Party holds a single seat majority on the Council. Word has it the other Party Councillors are in Brennan's pocket, but of course Frank Conroy was never for sale. For as long as your father sat on the Council Brennan sat on the land.

TESS But the ground shifted when Johnny was elected to replace him?

JOE So it seems. Around that time Johnny opened his auctioneering business. Pretty soon Brennan starts to put a bit of work his way. A house or two, a petrol station, a few industrial units — enough to help a young auctioneer make a name for himself in a tough game. But chickenfeed compared to what's coming if that land is rezoned and Brennan builds on it. (*Pause*) Looks like he might get his majority vote, doesn't it?

TESS Looks like the usual bucket of small town sleaze.

JOE With one difference. If your father becomes Taoiseach next week that story is going to mean a lot more than it does now. He's fighting Grogan on one issue, Tess. The last thing he needs right now is a scandal — quite literally on his own doorstep.

KATHERINE Then maybe you shouldn't write the story.

JOE That's called shooting the messenger, Katherine. Johnny's the problem here — not me.

KATHERINE Kilgallen is small beer, Joe. If Frank wins next week there's a chance to go after the real stuff.

JOE With respect, Katherine, Kilgallen *is* the real stuff. I hope Frank does win — but not at any price. I came to Seafield tonight to talk to Johnny. I had a suggestion to make — but, as you said, he wasn't interested in talking.

KATHERINE Maybe his father would be more receptive.

JOE We'll soon find out. One of his sidekicks calmed Johnny down and sent word the Minister would be happy to see me later. They asked me to wait for him here.

KATHERINE I see. Well, I'm sure it can all be sorted.

JOE I hope so.

STEPHEN (*Going back to work*) And there I was thinking you'd called by to see me.

JOE I'm glad I did see you, Stephen. (*Looking at* TESS) It's good to see you all again. I'm sorry about the

	circumstances.
KATHERINE	You're just doing your job, Joe. Frank is doing his, too. And for all the obstacles Mr Grogan has put in his way he's done a damned fine job. I know I don't need to remind you of that.
JOE	No, you don't.

STEPHEN *switches on the lights — as much to change the subject as anything else.*

STEPHEN	Da–daaah! What do you think, folks?
KATHERINE	They're lovely, Stephen. All we need now is a hoopla stall and we can have a carnival.
STEPHEN	Carnival is right, Ma. And much more, besides!
KATHERINE	I'm sorry?
STEPHEN	Halley's Comet, Ma! I'm blue in the face telling you about it.
KATHERINE	Of course. I'd forgotten.
STEPHEN	(*Looking out on the horizon*) Looks like the Met Office has, too. The forecast was for clear skies, Joe. I don't like the look of them clouds.
JOE	It might hold off.
STEPHEN	As Neville Chamberlain said about the Second World War. But we live in hope. Now, Tess — the mulled wine awaits!
TESS	What did your last servant die of?
STEPHEN	*Insubordination*!

TESS *smiles wryly at* STEPHEN, *then goes inside.*

JOE	I'm sorry. I know this is awkward, Katherine.
KATHERINE	Nonsense! You have nothing to be sorry for. Frank should be here soon.
JOE	Maybe this isn't the place to talk. You might tell him I'll give him a call in the morning.
KATHERINE	You'll stay right where you are. Stephen and I are not exactly spoiled for visitors these days, are we, Stephen?
STEPHEN	What's seldom is wonderful!

KATHERINE And I promise — not another word about anything but the good times. We did have plenty of
those once, didn't we, Joe?

JOE Yes. We did.

KATHERINE Then you'll stay?

JOE (*Smiling*) I'll stay. I could do with calling my office,
though. Would you mind if I used the phone?

KATHERINE (*Smiling*) I'm sure you remember where it is.

JOE I do.

JOE *exits.*

KATHERINE Tess's loss is Dublin's gain. That boy must break
hearts with every breath.

STEPHEN 'That boy' is thirty-six years old.

KATHERINE At my age that still qualifies. Poor Tess. Joe turning
up like this must have been quite a shock.

STEPHEN I get the feeling she's not alone on that score.

KATHERINE Johnny is a fool, Stephen — a boy dressed in a
man's suit. I know you don't like to talk about it
but he lost his innocence the night Laura died.
One way or another, we all did. Sometimes I sit at
her grave and envy her her peace.

STEPHEN You don't mean that, Ma.

KATHERINE (*Pause*) You're right, I don't. I'm just tired, that's
all.

STEPHEN That's allowed. It was a long night.

KATHERINE Something tells me it'll be a long night yet. I'll
rally again tomorrow, Stephen. I won't let your
father down, I promise you. But it's all cost so
much, hasn't it?

STEPHEN We've paid in full, Ma. It'll be worth it.

KATHERINE I hope so. (*Pause*) Coming up from the hotel, just
now, I was thinking of when he used to hold his
Constituency Clinics here in the house.

STEPHEN His 'petitioners', you called them.

KATHERINE (*Laughs*) That's right. And he was their healer.
D'you remember, Stephen? He'd station himself
in that makeshift office off the kitchen and all day

long they'd file in and unburden themselves.

STEPHEN I remember.

KATHERINE I think that was what he felt closest to. It was more than just about votes, Stephen — they were his *kindred*. (*Pause*) Johnny does those Clinics now from the Party office in Rathmore. They say your father is too busy with his Holy War on Grogan to be bothered, but I know it has nothing at all to do with that. What they loved him most for was that he was always truthful with them. In forty years I never heard him promise one of them something he couldn't deliver. The truth was his weapon and his armour, Stephen. He lost them both the night we let you lie for him. And he hates me for that as much as he hates himself.

STEPHEN He doesn't hate you, Ma. Now c'mon, this night was meant to be a celebration! What's that you promised Joe about the good times?

KATHERINE I try not to remember the good times. When I do it hurts too much. (*Pause*) I danced with your father tonight for the first time in four years. It was the first dance and the band insisted we dance alone. They turned down the lights, the mirror ball began to turn and everybody cheered as your father led me onto the dance floor. His old stalwarts gathered in a circle around us on the floor, Johnny and his cronies came in from the bar, the band struck up 'The Moonlight Serenade' and we began to dance. (*Pause*) I tried, Stephen. I tried so hard to make that moment what everybody in that hall wanted it to be — the warm and intimate embrace of a loyal and loving couple. But when I looked into your father's eyes all I could feel was absence; all we could see was the reflection of each other's guilt. (*Pause*) It was at that precise moment I recalled the presence of the Ministerial chariot in the hotel car park.

STEPHEN (*Embracing* KATHERINE) It's okay. Everything's going to be okay.

KATHERINE I miss him, Stephen. I miss my children.
STEPHEN Nobody's gone anywhere they won't come back from, Ma.
KATHERINE No?
STEPHEN No. I promise you that.

> STEPHEN *goes to the ghetto blaster and turns on Nat King Cole.*

(*As intro music plays*) We should dance.
KATHERINE I don't feel like dancing.
STEPHEN All the more reason. (*They begin to dance,* KATHERINE *with some reluctance*) There you go now. To the manner born. You just have to keep dancing. Just keep on dancing till the pain goes away. (*Pause*) That's it, Ma. We're getting the swing of it. Chin up, now. Eyes from the floor. Look up at the stars, Ma. (*And she does*) Stars for a star. Stars for my brightest star.

> *They dance on for a moment or two.* JOHNNY *enters from around the side of the house. Watches them dance.* STEPHEN *becomes aware of his presence. He stops dancing.*

JOHNNY Don't let me interrupt. Looks like a real cosy little scene you've got going there.
STEPHEN (*Turning off the tape*) Long time no see, Johnny.
JOHNNY Can't say that's bothering me. You can sure turn a step when you want to, though, Ma.
KATHERINE I'm out of practice.
JOHNNY You could have got plenty practice below in the hotel. You could have danced all night down there if you wanted to.
KATHERINE Maybe I didn't want to, Johnny.
JOHNNY I just called by to see if you were okay.
STEPHEN Ma is fine, Johnny.
JOHNNY Was I talking to you?
KATHERINE I'm okay, Johnny.

JOHNNY Good. Then maybe you'd like to come back down with me.

KATHERINE I don't think so.

JOHNNY I think you should, Ma. There's more TDs and Senators below in that ballroom than you'd see in the Horse Show House the night of an Ard-Fheis. And each and every one of them has a vote on whether Da gets to be Taoiseach next week. This gig is the last hurdle, Ma. And I'll grant you this: you didn't put a foot wrong all night.

KATHERINE Can you say the same, Johnny?

TESS *returns.*

JOHNNY Harrington had no business in that hotel tonight.

KATHERINE You know why he was there.

JOHNNY I know the bastard was lucky he didn't leave in an ambulance.

KATHERINE Joe Harrington is a decent man. Which is more than can be said for the company you were keeping.

JOHNNY I'm old enough to choose my own friends.

STEPHEN Maybe you should go back to them, Johnny.

JOHNNY Shut your trap, Spaceman. I've the car outside, Ma. If we hurry they'll think you just went to powder your nose.

KATHERINE I'm not going back there.

JOHNNY You owe him, Ma.

TESS Don't you think she's paid enough?

JOHNNY What would you know about that? You weren't here to know.

TESS That's right, I wasn't. But I can see the family business was in good hands in my absence.

JOHNNY Bloody sure it was. We couldn't all go running off to England like you did, could we, Tess? But then running away when the chips are down is the family sport in this house.

STEPHEN That's enough, Johnny. Go on home now.

JOHNNY This is my home. I'm Frank Conroy's son. Son and heir.

63

KATHERINE   That must make him very proud.

JOHNNY   More than can be said for your dancing partner here. Stevie here's a nobody now. Nothing but a lily-livered coward kept here out of the charity of my father's heart. But it won't always be like that. You remember that.

STEPHEN   I'll remember.

JOE *enters.*

JOE   Hello again, Johnny.

JOHNNY   What the fuck is he doing here?

KATHERINE   How dare you!

JOE   It's all right, Katherine.

JOHNNY   (*To* KATHERINE) You know what this bastard was up to in the hotel tonight. Digging for dirt the same as the rest of his scumbag trade. Well, you won't do it here, Harrington. Get out of our house before I throw you out.

TESS   Joe isn't going anywhere, Johnny.

JOHNNY   We'll see about that. You put the run on him once, Tess, and I'll do it again now.

KATHERINE   Over my dead body! Get out, Johnny! Get out and bring your foul tongue and your jackboot tactics with you.

JOHNNY   I'll go, Ma. But you remember what I said. You better figure out real fast whose side you're on.

KATHERINE   I know whose side I'm on. Can you say the same?

JOE   It's okay, Katherine. Johnny's right — I shouldn't have come back here. But what happened down at that hotel tonight is different. I'm entitled to ask a question.

JOHNNY   Who says?

JOE   Democracy says. You want me to spell it for you?

JOHNNY   (*Grabbing the lapels of* JOE's *jacket*) I can spell it, Harrington. And I know what it means, too. It's what people like my father give their lives protecting so that smart alecs like you get the right to destroy them. (*Releases* JOE. *Pushes him away*) With fucking hearsay.

JOE It's a bit more than hearsay, Johnny.

CONROY *enters. Looks at* HARRINGTON *and* JOHNNY.

CONROY I left as soon as I could. Are you okay, Katherine?

KATHERINE I'm fine. I'm sorry if I embarrassed you.

CONROY I shouldn't have put you through that charade. It won't happen again, I promise. (*Pause*) It's good to see you again, Joe. I'm sorry we didn't have the opportunity to speak at the hotel.

JOE I could see you were busy.

JOHNNY Harrington seems to have lost his way, Da. He was just leaving.

CONROY Joe is welcome in our house.

JOHNNY Not in my book, he isn't.

CONROY Your book doesn't count for very much just now.

JOHNNY What that bastard writes on Sunday might.

CONROY Maybe you ought to have given some thought to that before now. I understand you want to talk about Kilgallen, Joe.

JOE (*Glance to* JOHNNY) I don't want to spoil your night. We can talk in the morning.

CONROY If you don't mind I'd prefer to deal with it now.

KATHERINE I'll light the fire in the study.

JOE There's no need, Katherine. This won't take long. I didn't want to come down here, Frank. I rang Johnny's office three times this week. This could have been avoided if he'd taken my calls.

JOHNNY I have nothing to say to you, Harrington.

JOE We'll see about that in a minute. You know the story on Monday night's rezoning vote, Frank. The way I see it, what's happening on that Council is precisely the reason you're trying to put Emmet Grogan out to pasture next week. And that's why I'm here. This is your patch and Johnny is your son. I know you've got your eye on the bigger picture right now, but if you're going to take Grogan out you have to sort this first.

JOHNNY   Sort what, Harrington?

CONROY   Shut up, Johnny. (*Pause*) I appreciate your con-
cern, Joe. And your candour. As a Government
Minister I suppose my response should be a little
more circumspect. But to hell with that. (*Looking at*
JOHNNY) The proposed demolition of Kilgallen
House and the circumstances surrounding it are a
disgrace that shames everybody connected with it.

JOHNNY   It's a condemned building, Da.

CONROY   Yes. Condemned by wilful neglect and sharp practice. Let me spell this out, Joe. I was told about the
demolition order when I got back from Dublin last
night. I called the OPW this morning but, as the
house isn't listed, they say it's a matter for the
Council. I spoke to the County Manager this after-
noon asking for a stay of execution. The Manager
told me he was in possession of an order that
obliged him to knock the house.

JOE   He would say that, wouldn't he? But not if his
Councillors tell him otherwise.

CONROY   The legal position on that is unclear. I've sought
an opinion from the lawyers in my Department.

JOE   How long will that take?

CONROY   I don't know. A few days, I suppose.

JOE   You don't have a few days. Brennan was served
the demolition order yesterday. If that rezoning
goes through on Monday night he'll have a bull-
dozer on the land at first light on Tuesday.

CONROY   I'm doing all I can, Joe.

JOE   That may not be enough. (*Pause*) Johnny here can
do a lot more.

JOHNNY   Not for you I won't.

JOE   No. But maybe for your father — not to mention
the community you were elected to represent.

JOHNNY   I know who I represent.

JOE   I'm sure you do. And what you can deliver for
them, too.

CONROY   What are you getting at, Joe?

JOE   I would have thought that was obvious. Especially

to you, Frank. If that estate *isn't* rezoned on Monday Brennan's not going to be so anxious to knock the house — especially when he's obliged to foot the bill for the demolition. Everybody knows the sums. All it would take is one abstention to upset the apple cart.

JOHNNY Are you telling me how to vote?

JOE I am, Johnny. But then I'm not the only one who does that.

JOHNNY Fuck you!

CONROY Hold your tongue, boy!

JOHNNY You heard what he said, Da!

CONROY I told you to hold your tongue! (*Pause*) What exactly *are* you saying, Joe?

JOE That your son is in Paddy Brennan's pocket.

JOHNNY That's a lie, Harrington!

JOE Brennan's been priming Johnny for this vote since the night he took your seat on the Council. Monday is payback time.

JOHNNY That's a lie, Da, and you know it!

CONROY It's an extremely serious allegation.

JOE It is. And not just for Johnny.

CONROY Johnny knows how I feel about Brennan. I warned him that taking business from his like would leave him open to compromise and I regret he chose to ignore that warning. But that's his choice and he's entitled to make it.

JOE If I was Emmet Grogan I'd describe that as the sound of somebody washing his hands.

CONROY My hands are clean, Joe.

JOE Johnny's aren't. And he's your son.

CONROY I hardly think a few auctioneering commissions amount to a bribe.

JOE I think you know exactly what they amount to.

CONROY Be careful what you're saying.

JOE I'm watching every word. You've been around long enough to know Brennan is far too subtle for brown envelopes. 'Incentive' is the word I'd use, Frank. Brennan is planning to build a hundred-

and-twenty holiday homes on the estate if the
land is rezoned. And there's no prize for guessing
who's selling them.

JOHNNY How the hell do you know what he's planning?
Are you some sort of fortune-teller?

JOE I don't need to be, Johnny. I have your word for it.

Silence.

JOHNNY What do you mean, my word?

JOE Discretion isn't your strongest suit. I hear you've
been canvassing interest for houses that don't even
exist yet.

JOHNNY (*Stung*) That's called market research.

JOE Touting for cash to secure coastal view premium
sites is a little more than market research, Johnny.
A bit previous, I would have thought. But then, if
you can guarantee safe passage on rezoning and
planning permission, I guess you might as well be
getting on with it.

Silence.

CONROY (*To* JOHNNY) Is this true?

JOHNNY (*To* JOE) Who told you that?

JOE Let's just say I heard it on the wind, Johnny.

CONROY (*Shouts*) Never mind who told him! I asked you if
it was true.

JOE (*To* CONROY) You know it is, Frank. The same wind
blew all the way into your office.

CONROY I have no idea what you're talking about.

JOE No? Then it's my turn to spell it out. I got a phone
call last week from a man who said Johnny had
approached him a few weeks back about buying a
site at Kilgallen. There'd be no receipts, no paper-
work of any sort, just a five grand 'finder's fee'
that would secure a premium site with guaran-
teed planning approval. Unfortunately for you,
Johnny, you hit on the wrong man. Someone who

thinks a lot of your father. Not a Party stalwart, Frank, just an ordinary punter who said he admired what you were trying to do for his country and understood the implications of Johnny's little enterprise. He declined Johnny's offer, but he didn't leave it at that. That night he sat down and he wrote a letter. The letter was unsigned but its message was clear. The following morning he posted it to you.

CONROY   I never received that letter.

JOE   It was sent here by registered post — he has proof of delivery.

CONROY   You have my word, Joe. I never got that letter.

JOE   (*Looking at* KATHERINE) Somebody did.

Silence.

KATHERINE   I told you, I do have my functions, Joe. Like that letter, they're largely anonymous but I *do* play a part. I shield, I siphon, I prioritize and I protect. I thought I could protect you from this, Frank.

CONROY   By pretending it would go away?

KATHERINE   That's our second nature, isn't it? I did no more or less than you would. I spoke to Johnny, told him what I knew, warned him of the consequences and begged him to stop. I had no reason to think the matter wouldn't end at that.

JOE   Trouble is it didn't. Seafield's a small place. Two weeks after he sent the letter my friend heard Johnny was still touting. That's when he called me.

CONROY   I should have been told, Katherine.

KATHERINE   These days you're told what you need to know. I figured you could do without knowing your son was no better than the rabble you've spent your life fighting.

JOHNNY   (*To* KATHERINE) I'm not on trial here. (*To* CONROY) And, whatever you and your weasel friend here think of him, neither is Paddy Brennan. Maybe it's because you've been so busy with your moral crusade you've forgotten it, Da, but I was *elected* to that Council. No co-options, no sliding into his old man's chair for Frank Conroy's son. Just so everything was squeaky clean when you became the Minister for Public Morals I had to wait for an election and take my chances with the rest of them. Well, I did, didn't I? Only it wasn't Paddy Brennan who elected me, Da, but people who depend on the Brennans of this world for something else you and this bastard seem to have forgotten about — like a job, maybe, or a decent future in their own place.

KATHERINE Your father has dedicated his life to that purpose.

JOHNNY Eaten bread is soon forgotten. Some of those people say you're out of touch, Da — they say you've been so obsessed with filleting your own Party that you've taken your eye off what really matters.

CONROY By all accounts you've more than compensated.

JOHNNY Maybe I've had to. You think anyone gives a damn about Lord Kilgallen's eyesore? Did you see anybody shedding tears when your grand plan for a Community Park was scuppered, Da? I didn't. And you know why? Because people round here live in the dirt and dust of the real world. And you only get the licence to keep crying out in the moral wilderness as long as people like me live in that real world with them.

TESS Then you won't mind Joe letting them know you're on the make, will you, Johnny?

JOHNNY I'm an auctioneer. And a County Councillor. Not some spineless hack who trades in muckraking. If I make a few bob out of that land it's no more than I'm entitled to.

CONROY As long as you declare an interest in it.

JOE And declaring an interest means you abstain in Monday's vote. That's all I'm looking for, Johnny. I'll write everything I know about Kilgallen House for Sunday's paper and we'll all take the consequences, your father included. (*Pause*) But only if I have to. If that rezoning *doesn't* go through and the Council puts a stay on the demolition, then there won't *be* any story, will there? You have until tomorrow morning to let me know what you decide.

JOHNNY You'll be waiting.

JOE I can wait. Until midday, Johnny. No longer.

CONROY I'm not asking for your protection. You do your job as you see fit.

JOE This *is* as I see fit. You take Grogan out next week and you can put a stop to all the Brennans who prosper on Grogan's watch. To do that you don't need this getting in the way.

CONROY I'm not responsible for my son's probity.

JOE Then who is, Frank? Try telling that to Emmet Grogan — not to mention the Opposition. The fight's in your own backyard now and if you don't deal with it here you lose the right to point the finger anywhere else.

CONROY I won't tell my son how to vote.

JOE Why not? Everybody else does.

CONROY I won't. (*Looking at* JOHNNY) It's his decision.

JOE As I said, he has until midday tomorrow. If I don't hear from him I'll be inviting you to make a statement for Sunday's paper.

CONROY I've already given you one.

JOE You'll need to do better than that, Frank. Condemning what's happening here is one thing. Dealing with it is another.

CONROY What are you looking for?

JOE That's up to you. But you might like to make it clear that if that rezoning goes through on Monday and you're elected Taoiseach this week you'll replace the puppets on the Anti-Corruption Commission with people you can trust and send them down here on the first bus out of Dublin.

KATHERINE You want him to investigate his own son?

JOE If that's what it comes to. Kilgallen mightn't

amount to much in the grand scheme of things, Katherine, but it's all about perception, isn't it? (*To* CONROY) Investigate what's happening here and people will know it's the same law for everybody. Don't and you gamble on the last chance you'll ever have to make a difference.

> *Silence.*

CONROY Maybe I've gambled too much already. We reap what we sow, don't we, Katherine? (*Pause*) Looks like we both have a decision to make, Johnny.

JOHNNY I'm going back to the hotel.

CONROY I'd prefer if you didn't.

JOHNNY There's people down there need to be looked after.

CONROY It seems you've done more than enough of that already.

JOHNNY People with your future in their hands.

CONROY My future is in your hands now. Just as yours is in mine.

JOHNNY Because he says so?

CONROY Joe didn't bring it down to this. We did, Johnny — for better or worse.

JOHNNY I'm going back to the hotel. And you know why? Because I don't run away. Look around you, Da. Everybody in this yard went missing on you when it counted. Everybody but me. Maybe you forgot that. Maybe it's hard to see down into the dirt when you spend so long on the high moral ground, but I was here when you needed me. And whatever way it goes for you in Dublin next week when you walk out of that Party Room you're going to remember who was on your side and who wasn't.

TESS He already knows, Johnny. (*Looking at* CONROY) Maybe it's time you were told, too.

STEPHEN Leave it, Tess.

JOHNNY Told what?

KATHERINE Nothing, Johnny.

JOHNNY Told what, Tess?

STEPHEN There's nothing to tell, Johnny.

TESS There's the truth, Stephen.

STEPHEN Too late, Tess. Leave it now.

JOHNNY What truth?

CONROY (*Beat*) About me, Johnny.

KATHERINE Don't, Frank. I'm warning you. You'll destroy us all.

CONROY Look around you, Katherine. I've already done that.

JOHNNY What are you talking about, Da?

KATHERINE Go down to the hotel, Johnny. *Please*. I'll follow you down, I promise you.

TESS No! No more running away. It's time, Ma.

KATHERINE This is neither the time nor the place, Tess.

TESS Then where *is* the place? And when *is* the time? If Johnny walks out that door he'll never come back. But if he *is* corrupt, then this house is too. Every time I come home another little bit of us has broken away. There'll be nothing left, Ma.

KATHERINE So be it! That hurts, Tess — more than you'll ever know. But so be it. That's what we bought in for.

TESS I didn't 'buy in' for any of this. The man I was supposed to marry didn't either.

KATHERINE Is that what this is about? Revenge?

TESS (*Defeated by this*) No. Far from it. (*Pause*) You take care, Johnny.

TESS *begins to leave.*

JOHNNY Finish what you started, Tess.

TESS (*Stops*) No. Ma is right. It doesn't matter.

CONROY Nothing ever mattered more, Tess. This house *is* corrupt. But we haven't lost everything yet. Maybe the truth will heal us, Katherine.

KATHERINE The truth will cripple you.

CONROY We were crippled by a lie. If it's not too late I'll take a chance on the truth now.

STEPHEN We had a deal, Minister. You and me had a deal. I

kept my part of it.

CONROY   I know you did, Stephen. But I won't keep mine. Not any longer.

STEPHEN   Then you take the consequences.

CONROY   I will. (*Beat*) You were right, Johnny. You're not the one on trial here. I told Joe my hands were clean. Laura Gavin's blood is on my hands.

JOHNNY   What are you saying?

CONROY   It's me who's in the dock now, Johnny. I was driving the car the night of Laura's accident. It was me who ran away.

Silence.

JOHNNY   No. I don't believe that.

CONROY   It's true, Johnny.

Silence. JOHNNY, *clearly shocked, looks from* CONROY *to* STEPHEN *and then to* TESS.

JOHNNY   (*To* TESS) Did you know?

TESS   Nobody told me. (*Looking at* JOE) But I knew.

JOHNNY   Is that why you left?

TESS   Yes.

CONROY   I'm so sorry, Tess.

TESS   I know you are. But let's take the Acts of Contrition as read, Da. If you're in the dock, then you're not on your own. We all made choices and we've all paid the price. Johnny has a choice to make now.

JOHNNY   What do you think I'm going to do, Tess? Hotfoot it back to the hotel, grab a microphone and tell the Minister's adoring fans that their hero is a fraud and a hypocrite? Or maybe I'll go inside and give Emmet Grogan a call. Tell him to relax, Mr Whiter-than-white has got blood on his hands! What do you think, Joe? What would you do? Come to think of it — what *did* you do?

JOE   I didn't do anything, Johnny. I ran away, too.

JOHNNY   Oh yeah? You going to put that on the front page next Sunday? Or do you only do *big* stories, *important* stuff about gobshite councillors and what becomes of a ruin and a few acres of mud overlooking the sea? Tell me something, Minister? Tell me how you can stand in this yard and lecture me on declarations of fucking interest when you're the man that abandoned a dying girl and let your son do jail for it? I want you to tell me how you can do that?

CONROY   Practice, Johnny. Four years of practice.

JOHNNY   Fuck you! Fuck you, *Minister*!

CONROY   You get as angry as you like, Johnny — you're never going to hate me as much as I hate myself. I left more than Laura on the Sky Road that night.

JOHNNY   What did you leave, Minister — your briefcase?

CONROY   My good name. My self-respect. They're rotting in the same clay that buried Laura. I look in the mirror and there's nothing to see. When I speak my voice mocks me, points me to the blood on my hands that will never wash off. That's as it should be, Johnny. That's the least I should pay.

JOHNNY   Except you didn't pay. (*Looking at* STEPHEN) *He* did.

STEPHEN   My choice, Johnny.

JOHNNY   He didn't exactly get in your way, did he?

CONROY   (*Looking at* KATHERINE) Events, as they say, overtook us. I abandoned Laura and then I abandoned my son — one betrayal equal to the next. After that I had a simple choice to make. Wallow in shame or justify Stephen's sacrifice. In order to do so I've had to learn to live with my hypocrisy — to embrace it. I'm the consummate actor now, Johnny. I claim a moral authority I no longer possess, I preach what I believe but no longer practise. That's my atonement, Johnny.

   Silence.

JOHNNY I didn't need to know what you've just told me.

CONROY You did. Because you have a decision to make and you need to know how much is riding on it. I can't bring Laura back but I can, in some measure, redeem the debt I owe your brother. Taking out Grogan next week is just the next instalment. And that's where you come in.

JOHNNY You want me to pay your stinking debt?

CONROY I want you to help me pay it. It's your move first, Johnny. Give Joe a commitment to abstain in that vote, he'll drop his story and I'll go do battle with Grogan. If you don't he'll run with everything he has on you and then the next move is mine.

JOHNNY You pay your own debts. (*Pause*) I'm just sorry it wasn't you who died in that car.

JOHNNY *begins to leave.*

KATHERINE Where are you going, Johnny?

JOHNNY I'm going home.

STEPHEN This is your home.

JOHNNY (*Glancing to* CONROY, *then back to* STEPHEN) I hope you think he was worth it.

STEPHEN I do, Johnny.

JOHNNY *exits.*

CONROY You go write your story, Joe.

JOE This part was off the record.

CONROY The biggest scoop of your career.

JOE A career isn't everything, is it, Frank?

CONROY You think I don't know that?

JOE The deal stands with Johnny. I'll call him in the morning.

CONROY I think he's already made up his mind.

JOE We'll see.

CONROY Print and be damned, Joe. I already am.

JOE No. I'm not going to play your conscience on this one. We'll wait to hear from Johnny.

CONROY   I've already sacrificed one son — I'm not prepared
to do it again. If Johnny walks into the Council
Chamber on Monday and votes for that rezoning
I intend to withdraw from the leadership contest
and resign my seat.

JOE   That's up to you. Goodnight, Tess.

KATHERINE   (*As* JOE *begins to leave*) I envy you, Joe. (JOE *turns
back*) Your shining moral clarity. But not every-
body can afford the luxury. I know what you must
think of us. I know Tess and you paid as much as
anyone. But we're not evil. Did you think Grogan
and his like could be toppled by wishful thinking?
By piety and persuasion and high principle? They
have their place, but it's a brutal game, Joe. We
met fire with fire. We had to.

JOE   I hope it was worth it.

KATHERINE   I hope it will be.

JOE *exits.*

CONROY   Grogan can have the country, Katherine. If it's not
too late I want my family back.

KATHERINE   (*Pause*) I want *you* back — whatever happens now.
When you spoke in the hotel tonight I was re-
membering with every last detail a winter night
more than forty years ago. A parish hall at the foot
of the mountains. Twenty or thirty Party faithful
with mud on their boots and the hope in their
hearts that John Conroy's eldest son would be half
the man his father was. It was the first time I saw
you. And when you spoke it was with the same
passion and the same relentless conviction and,
whatever you say about where you left it, the
same luminous integrity that lit up that hotel
tonight. By the time you left that hall those people
would have followed you to hell. You'd given
them your heart — and I gave you mine the same
night. Those two nights are separated by more
than years, Frank. But I was looking at the same

man tonight. You remember that — and you do whatever you think now. I won't speak for our children but I stand where I always stood.

KATHERINE *exits.*

TESS That sounds like some kind of invitation.
CONROY Maybe. (*To* STEPHEN) Are you okay?
STEPHEN Never better. I'll give Johnny a shout in the morning. He might change his mind.
CONROY You think so?
STEPHEN I wouldn't put money on it. But you'd never know.

CONROY *begins to exit.*

Galileo. That fearless truth-searcher, observing the moon for the first time through the recently invented telescope, was pleased to note its surface pockmarked and flawed and not, as was widely held, perfectly smooth. (*Pause*) What an extraordinarily liberating discovery that must have been, Da. With what joyous abandon did the great astronomer bestride the cobbled streets of Naples, armed with the knowledge of such magnificent imperfection?

Silence.

CONROY Goodnight, Stephen. And thank you.
STEPHEN The pleasure was mine, Minister.

CONROY *exits.* STEPHEN *brings the ghetto blaster to the downstage 'observatory' chair. Then takes binoculars and points them skyward.* TESS *checks the bowl of mulled wine.*

TESS Any sign of Mr Halley?
STEPHEN Not yet. But the skies are clearing.

TESS   And the wine is still warm. Warmish. You want some?

STEPHEN   Why not? You didn't have the right to do what you just did.

TESS   No? (*As she hands him the glass*) You didn't have the right to give your life away.

STEPHEN   Maybe not. He's my father, Tess.

TESS   *Our* father.

STEPHEN   Who art in exile. I'd do it again.

TESS   I know you would. You crazy diamond, I know you would.

TESS *begins to leave.*

STEPHEN   You not waiting for Halley?

TESS   No. I have an early start in the morning.

STEPHEN   Back to London?

TESS   Yeah.

STEPHEN   Shame you can't stay longer.

TESS   Maybe next time.

STEPHEN   I hope so. (*As* TESS *opens the verandah door and without turning to her*) Heh, Tess. Something I want you to know.

TESS   What's that?

STEPHEN   Cassie. Cassiopeia. I let her go.

TESS   Yeah?

STEPHEN   In prison, ironically. I remembered what Joe said. That the end was never going to change no matter how many times I played it over in my head. So I let her go, Tess. It took a while, but I did.

TESS   I'm glad, Stephen.

STEPHEN   I miss her. I miss her real bad sometimes. But I know where she is. Just like I know where Laura is. (*Pause*) I couldn't see the sky when I was inside. It's not like an aeroplane when you can ask for an aisle seat. It didn't matter. Same as old Halley up there, just because you can't see it doesn't mean it's not there. And when I got out Cassie was waiting. Just where I thought I'd find her.

TESS   (*Smiles*) Goodnight, Stephen.

STEPHEN   It *is* a good night. The sky is clear, Tess. I can see everything.

> TESS *exits.* STEPHEN *turns on the ghetto blaster. Nat King Cole resumes as* STEPHEN *raises the binoculars to the sky as the general lighting fades, leaving only the glow from the carnival lights.*

Albireo. The double star. Big star, bright orange in the northern sky. Baby star, baby blue, nestling in Momma's warm glow.

> *He continues to look up as the carnival lights fade to black.*